BEARS

WRITER
Joni Phelps Hunt

SERIES EDITOR
Vicki León

PRINCIPAL PHOTOGRAPHER
Jeff Foott

ADDITIONAL PHOTOGRAPHERS
Tom Bean, John Cancalosi, J.M. Labat/Jacana, Wayne Lankinen,
Wayne Lynch, Tom McHugh, Mark D. Phillips, Art Wolfe

DESIGNER
Ashala Nicols Lawler

SILVER BURDETT PRESS

© 1995 Silver Burdett Press
Published by Silver Burdett Press.
A Simon & Schuster Company
299 Jefferson Road, Parsippany, NJ 07054
Printed in the United States of America
10 9 8 7 6 5 4 3 2 1

CLOSE-UP

A Focus on Nature

AB **SILVER BURDETT PRESS**

© 1995 Silver Burdett Press

Published by Silver Burdett Press.

A Simon & Schuster Company

299 Jefferson Road, Parsippany, NJ 07054

Printed in the United States of America

10 9 8 7 6 5 4 3 2 1

Library of Congress
Cataloging-in-Publication-Data

Hunt, Joni Phelps, 1956-

Bears: a global look at bears in the wild/ by
Joni Phelps Hunt; photographs by Jeff Foott.

p.cm. -- (Close up)

ISBN 0-382-24872-4 (LSB)

ISBN 0-382-24873-2 (SC)

1. Bears–Juvenile literature. [1. Bears.]

I. Foott, Jeff ill. II. Title. III. Series: Close up
(Parsippany, N.J.)

QL737.C27H863 1994

599.74'446--dc20

94-30911

CIP

AC

Where Brown Bears Live in North America

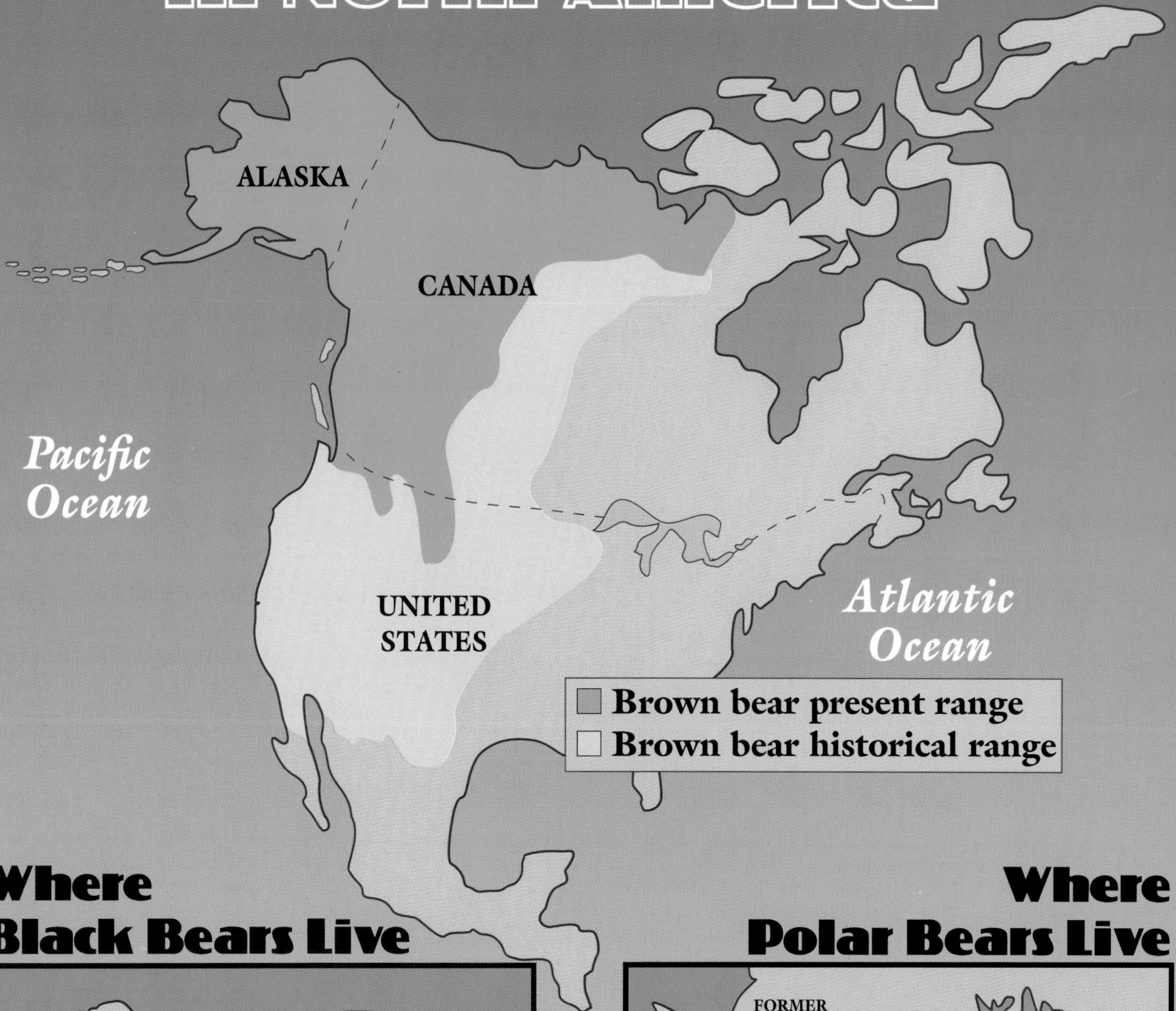

ALASKA

CANADA

Pacific Ocean

UNITED STATES

Atlantic Ocean

- ■ Brown bear present range
- □ Brown bear historical range

Where Black Bears Live

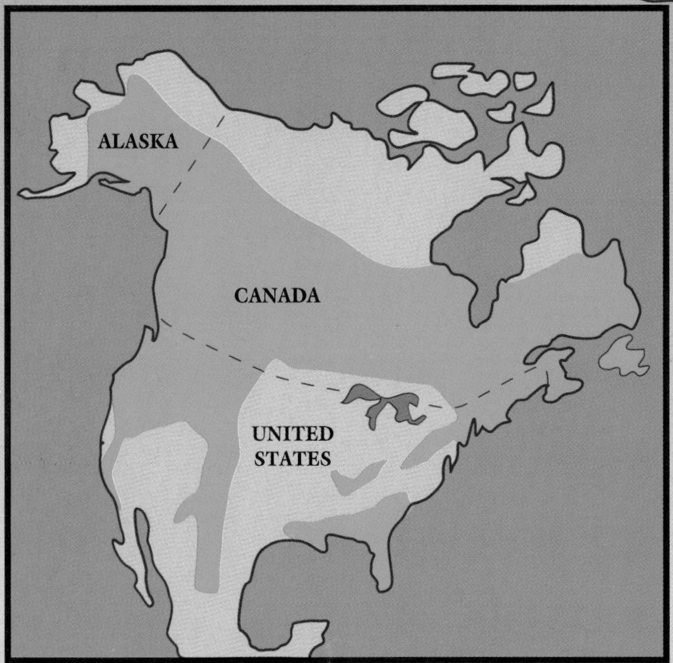

ALASKA

CANADA

UNITED STATES

Where Polar Bears Live

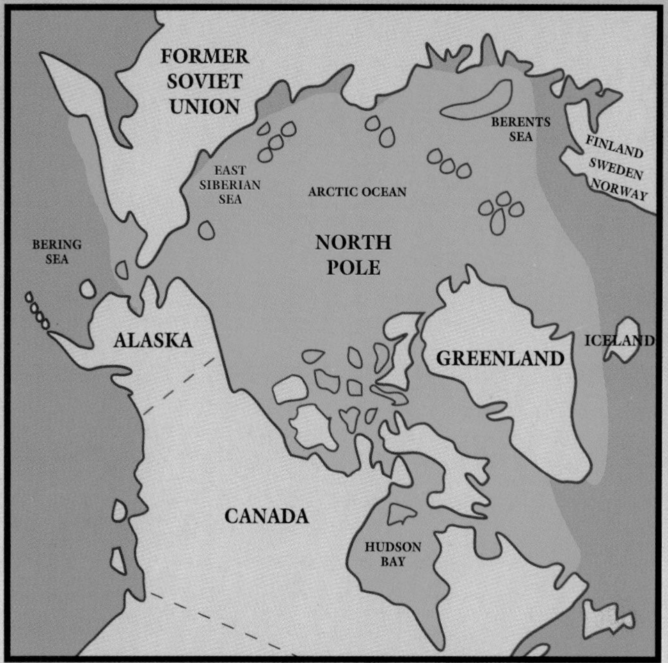

FORMER SOVIET UNION

BERENTS SEA

FINLAND
SWEDEN
NORWAY

EAST SIBERIAN SEA

ARCTIC OCEAN

BERING SEA

NORTH POLE

ALASKA

GREENLAND

ICELAND

CANADA

HUDSON BAY

BEARS

**need a lot
of room to roam –**

*For example, during its life
a grizzly bear may wander
a territory the size
of Rhode Island to find food,
winter dens, and mates.*

*Grizzlies and other bears
need the wide-open spaces
of wilderness areas like
Shoshone National Forest,
pictured here.*

MEET THE BEAR:

a curious, omnivorous mammal. An intelligent loner that's also a protective parent. Bears are resourceful: when stalking seals on the ice, a polar bear covers its black nose with a white paw to stay nearly invisible.

Sometimes they almost seem to have a sense of humor. A park ranger spraying an inquisitive black bear with red pepper spray to shoo it away from campers passes through the stinging cloud too. He goes to rinse his face in a nearby creek and hears campers laughing. The ranger looks up to see the bear beside him, washing its own face and looking over at him.

Bears roam with the seasons, foraging as foods become ripe and fattening up for winter hibernation. Except for mothers with cubs, bears are loners. When circumstances like plentiful food bring them together, they ignore each other.

Of the world's eight species of bears, seven are endangered, the eighth threatened. Their numbers have plummeted in the 20th century. Development of land and natural resources diminishes their territory. Poachers sell their body parts as trophies or for use as folk medicines.

Polar. Panda. Brown. Black. Sloth. Spectacled. Sun. Moon. All may soon be gone if we don't respect and protect their wildness.

KINDRED SPIRIT: "Bears are made of the same dust as we, and breathe the same winds and drink of the same waters. A bear's days are warmed by the same sun, his dwellings overdomed by the same blue sky, and his life turns and ebbs with the same heart-pulsings as ours."
— *John Muir*

BEAR FAMILY TREES

SOME 20 million years ago, the first bears are thought to have branched off from the dog family. Over time they became more like today's bears, the Ursus family, which has been around nearly three million years. In the past, these mammals lived on every continent except Antarctica and Australia. (Aussie koalas are actually marsupials, not bears.)

BROWN BEARS once ranged all through North America, Europe, North Africa, and Asia. Today they're gone entirely from places where they once thrived. England eliminated its bears by the Middle Ages. Brown bears were gone from the French Alps and much of the western United States by the 1930s.

North America's remaining 40,000 to 50,000 brown bears live mostly in northwestern Canada and Alaska. In the continental U.S., fewer than 800 roam isolated

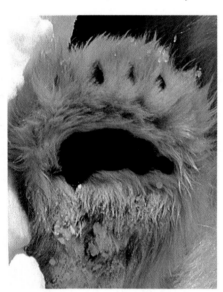

mountain areas of Idaho, Washington, Wyoming, and Montana. Grizzlies, named for the grizzled look of their dark coat with frosted tips, live in those states and other inland areas. Bears along the coast are known simply as brown bears. Kodiaks, the largest brown bears, came to live on islands in Alaska's Kodiak chain when they were separated from the mainland by a glacier about 10,000 years ago. Today's 2,500 to 3,000 Kodiaks have wider faces and larger skulls than their mainland relatives.

Europe's brown bears, hunted almost to extinction by the end of World War II, have made a modest comeback by living in remote areas and avoiding contact with humans. Most European countries now place strict limits or bans on bear hunting.

Asia has several brown bears, including those in India and China. One group of about 3,000 lives on Japan's Hokkaido Island. Because of limited space and food sources, hungry bears will attack livestock and even farmers. As a result, at least 10 percent of the island's bears are

BEAR FEET

How do you tell a brown bear from a black bear? Not by fur color. Check its paws instead. Tracks of a brown bear show claw marks; those of a black bear don't. Brown bears have long, straight claws and upturned noses, far left. They also have 42 teeth, above, and a hump of muscle over their shoulders. Black bears are smaller, with a straight nose and short, curved claws. Polar paws, near left, have short claws and thick fur for warmth and padding. The rough pads give traction on arctic ice.

killed each year. Researchers at Hokkaido University in Sapporo, Japan, study the animals in hopes of finding ways for bears and people and property to coexist.

Two separate species of **BLACK BEARS** – American and Asian – shared ancestors before the former migrated to North America across the Bering land bridge. American black bears once ranged across Canada and throughout forests in the U.S. and Mexico. Today they are confined to dense brush or forest and wilderness areas. Most numerous of the North American species at about one-half million, black bears live in Canada, Alaska, northeastern states, along the Pacific and Gulf coasts, and the Appalachian, Ozark, and Rocky mountains. A reforested area of New Jersey even has a few black bears.

Asian black bears are scattered in high mountain forests and coastal foothills from Iran east through the Himalayas, south into Laos, north through Tibet and into China. They're also found on Taiwan and two Japanese islands. Their popular name – moon bear – comes from the white or yellowish crescent-shaped markings on their chest fur.

Moon bears' fierce, short tempers and taste for grain and livestock cause frequent clashes with humans. As a result, laws to protect them aren't enforced. Hunting in Japan will likely eliminate moon bears within 20 years. The Chinese use their body parts in folk medicines and their paws in soups. In India, female moon bears are killed so that their captured cubs can be trained to dance and ride bicycles.

POLAR BEARS were once brown bears living in Siberia. More than 100,000 years ago, glaciers stranded some of them outside their forest homes. Gradually they adapted to harsh arctic weather and different food. They also changed color to blend with their new home. Eskimo or Inuit peoples hunted polar bears for meat and hides. The population begin to decline when fur traders arrived in the 17th century. By 1960 polar bears were nearly extinct.

BEAR GRUB

Bears spend most of their time looking for food. The biggest part of brown and black bears' diet – 80 percent – is plants. A North American black bear, above, feeds on buffalo berry in Grand Teton National Park. A cinnamon-colored black bear, right, pawses to drink in Yellowstone National Park.

SALMON LURE

Grizzlies catch salmon spawning in Alaskan rivers, at right, with several fishing techniques. Young adults allowed into the water often belly flop – and don't catch anything. More experienced adults either wade in and grab with their jaws, stand on shore and pin fish with a paw, or snorkel and grab fish underwater. Bears don't like their ears to get wet, so they keep them above water when snorkeling.

 N 1967, the countries where polar bears make their home drew up a conservation treaty to protect them. Today polars live on sea ice along the Arctic Ocean coast and the shores of Alaska, Canada, Greenland, Norway, and the former Soviet Union.

Powerful swimmers, polars can easily paddle 100 miles. They also hitch rides on icebergs, traveling to Iceland or even as far as Japan. In Greenland and around Canada's Hudson Bay, the bears spend summer on dry land, napping in beds of peat moss.

Heavy mists and rains shroud bamboo and coniferous forests in the mountains of China's Sichuan province, home to **GIANT PANDA BEARS**. Of the estimated 750 pandas in the wild, more than half live in 12 reserves set aside for their protection. Farming, logging, and building have eliminated much of their habitat. Also, supplies of bamboo, their main food, disappear every 40 to 120 years. After bamboo flowers and seeds, it dies. New shoots grown from the seeds may take 10 to 15 years to reach panda-food size. When two species of bamboo died off in the mid-1970s, at least 138 pandas died.

The Chinese consider the bears a national treasure. Since 1987, a death penalty awaits anyone convicted of killing giant pandas or smuggling their skins. Work to save this highly endangered species from extinction is done at a breeding and research center in the Wolong Reserve.

SPECTACLED BEARS, named for light markings around their eyes, are the only bears found in South America. About 2,000 inhabit dense mountain forests of the Andes in western Venezuela, Colombia, Ecuador, Peru, Bolivia, Chile, and coastal desert in Peru. Farming has reduced their habitat and food supply. When hungry spectacled bears eat corn crops, farmers apply pesticides to kill members of this endangered species.

With a mane of shaggy black hair, **SLOTH BEARS** live in both thorn forests and wet rainforests of India, Sri Lanka and Nepal. Large-scale cutting of these forests has caused a drop in the number of bears to about 7,000.

Named for the yellow splash of fur on their chest, **SUN BEARS** or Malay bears are also endangered in their diminishing rainforest homes in Thailand, Burma, Sumatra, Borneo, Java, the Malay Peninsula, and India. Although laws protect them, poachers kill female sun bears and capture the cubs for pets.

NAPTIME: When salmon are plentiful, bears eat only the most nutritious parts of the fish, the skin and eggs. These hold high amounts of fat, helping bears put on weight for winter sleep. Partly eaten fish go to gulls and younger bears.

BEAR BODIES

WHATEVER their color or size, bears' basic shape – big and stocky – stays the same. Sun bears, the smallest species, weigh about 100 pounds and measure four feet when standing on hind legs. The largest recorded bear, a polar, tipped the scales at 2,200 pounds and measured over 12 feet tall. The usual size for adult male polars is 1,000 pounds and just under ten feet.

Black bears range from a low of 125 pounds, 4½ feet to 600 pounds, six feet. Their size depends on how much food they're able to find. An average adult weighs 300 to 400 pounds and stands about five feet. Females usually are one-third smaller than males. Adult grizzly bears weigh between 300 and 850 pounds and stand up to nine feet tall. Kodiak brown bears reach 1,100 to 1,500 pounds. Giant panda, spectacled, sloth, and moon bears all average about 250 pounds and five to six feet in length.

A giant panda's black and white body blends with the snow and shadows of the bamboo forest. Its fur is coarse on the outside and

POLAR FARE

A polar bear's diet includes seaweed, above, and seals, top right. Polars hunting for a seal meal are often followed by an arctic fox, lower right, which feeds on the remains. When seals are scarce, a polar bear may dine instead on a fox that trails along too close.

dense and woolly underneath to keep it warm. An old Chinese word for panda, Bei-shing, means white bear. Chinese legend says the fur of giant pandas was once all white. A panda cub, playing with a young girl, was attacked by a leopard. The girl fought to protect the panda, but died of wounds she received. To honor her bravery and show their grief, pandas wore black on their arms, legs, and shoulders. The tears they cried for her turned their eyes, noses, and ears black.

Where an American black bear lives may determine its fur color, according to bear researcher Dr. Charles Jonkel. After winter denning, hungry black bears find a new supply of plant food on sunny south-facing slopes. West of the Mississippi River, cinnamon and other light-colored black bears feed longer on the hot hillsides than those with black fur, Jonkel found. In the cooler eastern U.S., as well as Washington state's wet Olympic Peninsula, black bears are all black. In the drier Cascade Mountains of Washington state, nearly 60 percent of the black bears have brown fur.

Another in the black bear family, the rare bluish-gray

glacier bear appears only in central Alaska and the Yukon. The bear blends well into its habitat, making it difficult to find (or hunt). Also rare is the beige-colored Kermode. These seldom-seen "ghost" bears live only in three remote areas of British Columbia. Canadian law forbids hunting them.

Members of the brown bear family change color too. They can be blue-black in Tibet, reddish in China, silver-tipped in North America, and tan elsewhere.

Even the once-brown polar bear isn't actually white. Its fur appears as pure white, yellowish, bluish, or gray. Since each hair is clear and hollow, the coat color changes as light and surroundings change. In summer when algae can grow in the hollow hairs, polars sometimes look green. Each hair, filled with air, adds buoyancy in water. The hairs also act as solar heat panels as they trap and conduct the sun's rays to the bear's black skin. That and a thick layer of fat help keep a polar bear warm in subzero temperatures.

A bear has a long body, short legs, a large head, small eyes and ears, and a stubby tail. Although it appears clumsy and slow, a brown bear can run up to 40 miles per hour. Large teeth both catch live prey and chew plant material. Growth rings in the teeth reveal a bear's age. In the wild a bear may live 30 years, but that is rare. Most black bears live only about ten years, polar bears less than 25.

Bears walk and run on all four feet, flat-footed and pigeon-toed. They stand on hind legs only to reach food, watch what arouses their curiosity, play, or fight. Five toes on each foot have curved claws, usually longer on the hind feet. They use their front paws to climb, find food, and strike prey or foe. When looking for food, the paws dig and lift logs and rocks. Small objects are handled between the claws and footpad.

GROUP DYNAMICS: Normally solitary bears come together to fish at McNeil River in Alaska. They follow a pecking order, with older, dominant bears taking the best fishing sites below the waterfalls. Those under six years must wait on the sidelines until their elders are full.

FIRE & ICE: A fiery arctic sunset lights up the clear, hollow hairs of a polar bear's fur. Built to survive the harsh arctic climate, everything but the nose and foot pads is covered with dense fur. A two- to four- inch layer of fat keeps the bear warm and adds buoyancy in water.

Only pandas have a sixth toe on their forepaws. An extension of the wrist bone, it works like an opposable thumb and is invaluable in handling the sturdy bamboo they feed on.

As far as bear researchers can tell, the five senses seem well-developed in most species. Naturalists and hunters used to think bears had poor eyesight because they approach unfamiliar objects. Now it's believed curiosity brings bears in for a closer look. Bears can catch moving prey and are active in daylight and darkness, indications of good sight. Only the giant panda and sloth bears are thought to have poor vision.

Smell often tells a bear more about an object than sight. Its keen sense of smell detects food several miles away and the scent of a human up to one mile upwind. Some researchers believe that polar bears can smell a seal 20 miles away or in a den under three feet of snow. Bears can also hear human conversation at 80 yards, and the click of a camera shutter at 14 yards.

WHAT DO BEARS EAT?

BEARS ARE omnivorous, meaning they feed on both plants and animals. The amounts in their diet vary by species and what's available seasonally. Bears stay within a territory – their home range – as they move between higher and lower elevations and follow food ripening on plants. They travel through remote swamps and forests on well-worn trails. The trails often have grooves in the soil for each bear's foot to step where thousands of its forebears walked.

Typically, one male bear's home range overlaps that of other males and several females. Territory is limited by the amount of wilderness habitat available and the number of bears sharing it. In the Yukon, for example, home range for a male brown bear is about 250 square miles and for a female about 45. An American black bear makes its home over 10 to 52 square miles. A giant panda in China's Wolong Reserve lives within only 1½ to 2½ square miles and shares all or part of that area with other pandas.

Polar bears range throughout the Arctic over some 20,000 square miles. They consume far more meat than

CUBBYHOLE
Bear cubs are born during winter in dens dug into snow, left inset, in caves, or in hollow trees, left. No bigger than a navel orange, the tiny cubs must gain weight and wait for their fur to thicken and eyes to open before leaving the den, usually 10 to 12 weeks. They continue to nurse, above, for more than a year. Meanwhile cubs sample other foods their mothers show them.

other bears. Finding a hole in the ice, a polar waits for a ringed seal to poke its nose up for air. The bear grabs the seal's head with its jaws and pulls the heavy animal, as much as 250 pounds, out of the water. Seals on top of the ice are also targets. While a seal naps briefly, a polar inches along the ice toward it. When the seal wakes, the bear stops, motionless. The polar may even cover its black nose with a white paw as camouflage. When a few yards away, the bear leaps and captures the seal.

Polar bears also feed on beached whales, walruses, fish, shellfish, sea birds and eggs, foxes, and young or injured reindeer, caribou, and musk ox. Plants in their diet include seaweed, summer berries, and grass. An adult polar bear's stomach can hold more than 150 pounds of food.

Brown bears emerge from winter dens in April without much appetite. They start slowly drinking water and nibbling new shoots of grasses. Bear researchers think a few light meals get their digestive system working after their winter fast. They may forage for leftovers like fall berries or fruit hidden in the snow, then look for meat from animals that didn't survive the winter. Brown bears

BEAR LAIR: After leaving the birthing den, female polar bears often dig shallow, temporary shelters in the snow. This mother blocks the wind and offers a warm place to snuggle while her cubs rest. She's protective, guarding her young from wolves or other bears.

GO FISH: Cubs mimic their mother's every move as she teaches them how to fish. Their red noses show that they've already sampled some salmon. A gull waits for leftovers.

rarely kill healthy deer, moose, elk, or caribou, but they will prey on young or injured animals.

To find food, brown bears travel from den areas to coasts or valleys. In spring and summer, their diet expands to include small mammals, insects, bird eggs, and fresh berries. In coastal areas they feed on shellfish and fish washed ashore. In Siberia, Canada, and Alaska, they catch river salmon for three to four weeks during summer. A grizzly consumes about 35 pounds of food a day and up to 90 pounds before hibernating. Although equipped with the long claws and teeth of a meat eater, only about 20 percent of a brown bear's diet is meat. The rest is plants.

Nicknamed the "four-footed garbage disposal," North American black bears have about the same ratio of plants to animals in their diet as brown bears do. They'll eat anything, but they prefer sweets and meat. As with browns, black bears break their winter fast with an appetizer of tender greens. This course is followed by rodents, berries, roots and bulbs, nuts, wild fruit, fish, frogs, bees, beetles, and more. One black bear with a sweet tooth may open six beehives to get its fill of honey. Its thick coat dulls the sting from angry bees. Young or injured moose, elk, mountain sheep, and deer also fall prey to the black bear.

Their scavenger ways lead black bears to sample the contents of backpacks, tents, barns, cabins, and henhouses. It's not unusual to see a bear's rump sticking out of a trash can or even a chimney. Once developing a taste for human food or domestic animals, black bears can rarely be stopped from going after more. In national parks or areas where bears and people are in close contact, problem bears often have to be trapped and relocated, reeducated, or killed.

Asian black bears feed on insects, fruit, berries, honeycomb, and nuts. They often sit high in a tree, bending branches with fruit toward them to form a nest.

ROUGHHOUSE

As cubs and young adults, bears wrestle playfully with their siblings. They hug, slap, nip, and growl. They play tag and turn somersaults by holding onto their own feet. Polar cubs learn to slide down glaciers and rock small icebergs, knocking other bears off.

Once in a while two adult male polar bears pair up to travel, feed, and play together, above. Two grizzlies, left, play-fight in Alaska's McNeil River.

In India and Tibet, they are considered pests for killing sheep, goats, and cattle. They are killed for feeding in the grain fields of Indochina and for peeling bark from trees earmarked for the timber industry in Japan. (American black bears are also killed for destroying timber.)

Spectacled bears' diet includes fruit, honeycomb, sugarcane, corn, palm nuts, and bromeliad hearts. They also hunt rabbits, deer, birds, and llamas. Considered a nuisance and a threat to corn crops and domestic cattle, spectacled bears are often killed or poisoned by angry farmers.

Sloth bears consume ants, termites, eggs, plants, fruit, berries, honey, and carrion. A sloth bear digs at a hard termite mound with its long claws until it breaks, and then blows heavily to clear dust and debris. Using its flexible muzzle and mouth with no front teeth like a vacuum cleaner wand, the sloth bear sucks up a meal of termites. In India during spring, sloth bears compete with people for the flowers of the Mohwa tree. The bears favor the flowers, which townspeople collect to make an alcoholic drink.

Sun bears use their long tongues to seek out insects. They round out their diet with snails, eggs, lizards, rodents, fruit, and honeycomb.

Although giant pandas will eat meat, more plentiful bamboo is their main food. With their strong teeth, pandas can munch 45 pounds of leaves, shoots, and stalks over a 14-hour period. When not eating, they rest or sleep in two- to four-hour shifts. Panda's digestive tracts are short, like other meat eaters. They receive little nourishment from bamboo, so they must eat almost continuously to survive. When available, pandas also eat fish, pikas, rodents, flower bulbs, vines, and honey.

BEAR BEHAVIOR

BEARS ARE keenly aware of the world around them and investigate anything unfamiliar. Adult bears – except females with cubs – almost always live alone. But they keep close tabs on each other by a system of scent marks, droppings, tree scratches, and footprints. When circumstances like large quantities of seasonal fish or berries bring many bears together, they behave in ways scientists call ignoring behavior and dominance hierarchy.

POLAR PLUNGE

A mother and cubs leap from sea ice, left. Polars paddle with their front feet and steer with the rear. With their Frisbee-sized paws, they can swim for ten hours – and up to 60 miles – without rest. Polar bodies are well suited for diving to depths of 15 feet for mollusks and seaweed. The bear shuts its ears and nostrils. A clear third eyelid protects the eyes, but allows the bear to see underwater. Finally, blood vessels shrink, holding enough oxygen for the bear to stay underwater about two minutes.

PANDA PUZZLE

When a giant panda bear, right, was first seen outside of China in 1936, scientists thought it might instead be a raccoon like the lesser or red pandas, above. Both pandas feed on bamboo and have long wrist-bones that work like thumbs to grip the plant. For now, giant pandas are considered bears. Some researchers think giant pandas should be in a family of their own.

The Chinese have rescue plans for giant pandas during bamboo shortages: set out food for hungry bears and carry them out of their mountain homes to stations where they can be fed. Meanwhile researchers develop new types of bamboo and coax pandas to feed on other foods, such as wheat.

A BEAR ARRIVING at Alaska's McNeil River during the salmon spawn appears to ignore others already fishing. Observers can tell the bear knows exactly where they are, however, by its route, posture, and behavior. The bear doesn't look directly at other bears, looking instead to the side. A direct stare would indicate a challenge and could easily lead to a fight.

Because they try to avoid fighting, bears develop a hierarchy or pecking order. The largest male bears wield the most status, then females with cubs, and other adult males. Single females and young adults place lowest on the totem pole. In a confrontation, males will defer to females with cubs because mothers fiercely defend their young. When it's unclear which bear is dominant, they test each other's strength with short fights or threat displays. As you might expect, dominant bears take the best fishing spots.

Adult male bears also fight over females during breeding season. A North American pair mates during a few days in summer, and the male then leaves. Development of the female's fertilized eggs is delayed up to five months after mating. That way the embryo develops and the cubs are born during winter denning. The female raises the cubs alone. Bear researchers think that sun and Asian black bears raise cubs with both parents present.

WINTER DENNING

MOST BLACK and brown bears in temperate climates retreat to a den to avoid harsh winter weather and food shortages. Unlike other true hibernating animals, bears can be awakened from sleep and their body temperatures stay fairly high. This modified version of hibernation, or torpor, allows them to care for cubs and quickly react to danger.

Bears prepare for a long winter nap in late summer by increasing their body fat. Grizzlies may eat up to 20,000 calories a day to accumulate six to ten inches of fat. American black bears can gain 30 pounds a week. Dens are made in caves, thick bushes, hollow trees, under rocks, or in a hole dug into the ground or ice. The same dens are often used each year.

Pregnant females find or make larger dens than other bears. They add more grasses and leaves for a cozier nest. Pregnant bears and those with first-year cubs enter dens earlier, usually mid-September, and leave later, sometime in May, than the others.

How can a bear hibernate for a period lasting from five to eight months without food or water? Its body systems slow down. The bear's heart rate drops from the usual 40 to 50 beats during a summer nap to between 8 and 20 beats per minute. It breathes half as much and loses one quarter of its weight. The bear's body burns about 4,000 calories a day, breaking down fat reserves to supply nutrients and water. Sometimes it shivers to keep warm.

Brown and black bears in mild climates and polar bears don't hibernate. Instead they may sleep for a short time, wake, feed, and sleep again. The other species – giant panda, sloth, sun, and spectacled bears – also skip winter hibernation. Food is plentiful year round, so they don't accumulate fat reserves. They may retreat to a den for several days' sleep or the birth of young, but they are soon out and foraging.

During spring and summer some bears make daybeds in bushes or shallow holes. Located near food sources, beds serve as crash pads after meals. Asian black, sun, and spectacled bears make nests in trees. The sloth bear, which doesn't make a nest, snores loudly wherever it decides to nap.

FURBEARERS

Short, thick fur repels rain and mud off the seldom-seen sun bear, left, in its tropical Asian home. Despite a shaggy coat, the sloth bear, above, naps in full sun in its home in India.

Both species can be fierce. A tiger won't tangle with a sun bear. Elephants tremble from fear of a sloth bear poised to attack.

Sloth bears squeal, yelp, roar, and gurgle. They also hum and buzz while sucking a paw.

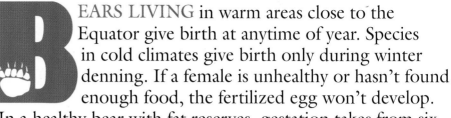

CUBS

BEARS LIVING in warm areas close to the Equator give birth at anytime of year. Species in cold climates give birth only during winter denning. If a female is unhealthy or hasn't found enough food, the fertilized egg won't develop. In a healthy bear with fat reserves, gestation takes from six to eight weeks, ten weeks for polar bears.

A female brown bear, weighing about 400 pounds, gives birth to a cub weighing only about ten ounces. A newborn panda weighs four ounces, a polar about 20. Averaging two to a litter, cubs have sparse fur and are blind for several weeks. Their mother licks them, nurses them, and keeps them warm. Not until their eyes open and fur becomes thick can the cubs leave the den, usually in 10 to 12 weeks.

Once they're out in the world, cubs become their mother's shadows as she teaches and protects them. Perhaps the greatest danger comes from adult male bears who sometimes try to kill and eat cubs. Cubs are also vulnerable to the same predators as adults, plus coyotes and harsh storms. Studies find 10 to 40 percent of cubs are killed in their first 18 months. More than 50 percent die by their third year. Researchers believe this may be nature's way of reducing overpopulation.

Cubs that don't obey their mother's commands to climb a tree or to come down get spanked or cuffed. As they get older they play with siblings, their mother, and alone. They learn to fish, eat different foods, and roam where their curiosity takes them. Young polar cubs accompany their mother on a slow long-distance trip across water. They make stops to nap on land. If they become too tired in the water, cubs ride on their mother's back. Along the way they watch and learn as the female catches seals for food.

Near the end of their first year, brown, black, and polar cubs enter a winter den with their mothers. By their second summer, the youngsters spend 90 percent of their time foraging. During that summer (the third summer for brown and polar bears), mothers force the cubs to go out on their own. The adult females mate again then or during the following summer.

TREE HOUSES

On opposite sides of the globe, the South American spectacled bear, below, and Asian moon bear, right, live in dense forests. Spectacled bears make daybeds in fruit trees, bending branches under them to form a nest, then stripping off the fruit. Moon bears' strong, curved claws give them a leg up when climbing trees.

DON'T FEED THE BEARS

A peanut butter and jam sandwich left on a picnic table equals two days of foraging. Bears looking for easy-to-get human food lose their fear of humans and are more likely to attack. Such problem bears have to be relocated, reeducated, or killed.

The good news: the average North American is 374 times more likely to be struck by lightning and 90,000 times more likely to be killed by another person than by a black bear.

ENEMIES

AS ADULTS, bears have few natural enemies. But the awkward stage between cub and adult is full of danger. Young adults don't yet have a home range and must avoid older, more dominant bears. Wolves and hunters with dogs also threaten. Usually by the time a bear reaches age five, its size and experience help it survive longer.

Adult bears chase other bears of the same species out of their territory. Two different species can share the same area as long as they stay separated. Scent markings help keep grizzly and American black bears apart. If they do meet accidentally, the black bear will be injured or killed. Russian brown bears flee from wolves and wild dogs, which harass and even kill bears. In Asia and India, tigers are deadly foes of sloth, black, and brown bears. Those in southern regions are in danger from snakes. Killer whales and large bull walruses occasionally kill polar bears. The greatest danger to all bears, however, comes from man.

BEARS & MAN

MAN HAS a checkered history with bears. Stone Age hunters and tribal cultures showed respect. To many, the bear served as a messenger between the spirit world and theirs. Going into a den each winter, the bear was thought to die and be reborn in spring. Legends of prehistoric cultures tell of people becoming bears, or bears people, and imparting knowledge of the forest.

On the other hand, ancient Romans and the English exploited bears, pitting them against gladiators and dogs as sport. Trained bears have long performed in traveling circuses. During westward growth, American settlers killed bears as nuisances to farming and livestock. As the country developed, prime habitat disappeared and bear numbers plummeted. Bears retreated to isolated mountains and swamps.

A romanticized version of bears entered popular culture in 1902 when U.S. President Theodore Roosevelt refused to shoot a black bear chained to a tree. The event received much attention, and toys made to honor the event were named teddy bears.

BEARING UP

Each winter when Canada's Hudson Bay freezes over, polar bears go onto the ice to hunt seals and replenish their fat reserves. With the spring thaw, bears hitch rides on ice floes to the bay's southern shore.

They walk inland for the summer. As the season changes, polars walk the 800 to 900 miles back to the northwest coast where the bay refreezes. Some 600 to 1,000 polar bears assemble along 100 miles of coast every November.

The town of Churchill prepares for the bears' arrival with safety classes and a holding area for troublesome bears. Tourists and photographers flock to the area to ride a tundra buggy, left, to view the polars.

As wild animals, bears can be dangerous. Usually, though, they just want to be left alone. If a grizzly sees, hears, or smells humans, it's likely to leave the area. If it's startled or approached, it may appear aggressive in self defense. Threat signals from a black bear include bellowing, sniffing, huffing, and staring. A bear may advance in a bluff charge, huffing with an open mouth, and then leave.

A U.S. computer database called Bear Information Management System (BIMS) keeps track of bear and human encounters. Specialist Dr. Charles Jonkel conditions problem bears to avoid people by using a cayenne pepper spray. Only one in 15 of his "bear school" graduates gets into trouble again.

The world's bears are all endangered or threatened, and their future is uncertain. "When they come into direct contact with humans, bears usually suffer," says mammal expert Michael Dee. If given a chance, Dee believes bear populations can rebound. First, bears require little or no contact with humans. They need protection against illegal hunting. They need spacious habitats that provide enough food and opportunities to meet other bears bringing new blood into the gene pool.

Even if humans do their part, bears still face problems. Polars rebounded by efforts of several countries. But recent computer projections show that global warming – by as little as one degree – will mean their end.

Polars in Hudson Bay feed for six weeks in winter when seals are plentiful, storing fat reserves. When sea ice breaks in July, they're forced ashore until November when it refreezes. On land the bears live off fat reserves. A rise in earth's temperature will cause sea ice to break sooner and freeze later. Researchers believe the polars' reserves won't last even an extra two weeks.

So what can we do to help bears? Working to have a healthier planet helps all species, not just polars. Global warming can be reduced by driving cars less and burning fewer fossil fuels. When camping in bears' habitat, leave them alone and keep food out of their reach.

No matter how adorable they may look, bears are wild animals. To survive, they must stay that way.

LEARNING TO COEXIST

Humans and bears can learn to live together, but it takes effort on both parts. In Alaska's Brooks Camp, plentiful trout and salmon lure brown bears and fishermen. Rangers teach bear etiquette to visitors: make noise walking in the forest, keep at least 50 yards away, yield the right of way. Bears, in turn, learn people aren't dangerous and pass the lesson to their young.

Another successful mixing of man and bear is Alaska's McNeil River, above and right.

ABOUT THE PHOTOGRAPHERS

Jeff Foott, whose captivating photos of North America's bears appear in these pages, spends many a cold day and night pursuing his subjects. Among the highlights of 20-plus years photographing black, brown, and polar bears, Jeff counts seeing the northern lights and being bluff charged by a bear. His award-winning films about bears and other nature subjects are shown on public television. Jeff's still photographs appear in *National Geographic*, *Audubon*, and other periodicals and books.

With his 32 images in *Bears*, Jeff captures seldom-seen behaviors of bears in the wild as they feed, play, explore, and interact in large groups and small family units.

An additional 11 images by other photographers provide a look at five bear species outside of North America. All photos not listed below are by Jeff Foott.

Tom Bean/DRK Photo: page 22 inset
John Cancalosi/DRK Photo: page 35
J.M. Labat/Jacana/Photo Researchers: page 39
Wayne Lankinen/DRK Photo: page 2
Wayne Lynch/DRK Photo: page 22
Tom McHugh/Photo Researchers: pages 36, 38
Mark D. Phillips/Photo Researchers: page 37
Art Wolfe: front cover, pages 32, 34

ABOUT THE AUTHOR

It was inevitable that Joni Phelps Hunt write a book called *Bears*. Her fascination with them spans three decades. In the meantime she's written *The Desert*, *A Chorus of Frogs*, and *A Shimmer of Butterflies* for Blake Publishing. Joni sends hugs to all of her bears – especially Les and Jamie.

SPECIAL THANKS

Brian W. Cahill, Ranger, Prairie Creek Redwoods State Park, California
Michael Dee, Curator of Mammals, Los Angeles Zoo
Jeff Foott
Dr. Charles Jonkel, University of Montana

TO LEARN MORE

• Write your state (U.S.) or provincial (Canada) wildlife office.
• Great Bear Foundation, P.O. Box 2699, Missoula, Montana 59806. Works to protect and conserve bears of the world and their habitats.
• International Association for Bear Research and Management. Check the National Wildlife Federation's Conservation Directory at your local library for the current address.

BOOKS

• *Bear Attacks: Their Causes & Avoidance*, by Stephen Herrero (Lyons & Burford, 1988)
• *Bears of the World*, by Terry Domico (Facts on File, 1988)
• *Grizzly Years: In Search of the American Wilderness*, by Doug Peacock (Henry Holt and Company, 1990)
• *Polar Bears*, by Ian Stirling (University of Michigan Press, 1988)
• *The Sacred Paw: The Bear in Nature, Myth, and Literature*, by Paul Shepard and Barry Sanders (Viking, 1985)

FILMS

• *The Bear* (RCA/Columbia Pictures Home Video, 1989). Rated PG.
• *Bears: Kings of the Wild* (Britannica Films, 1982, 23 min.)
• *The Grizzlies* (National Geographic, 1987, 60 min.)
• *Grizzly and Man: Uneasy Truce* (National Audubon Society, 1988, 60 min.)
• *Polar Bear Alert* (National Geographic, 1982, 60 min.)
• *Polar Bears and Their Frozen World* (Britannica Films, 1989, 16 min.)
• *Save the Panda* (National Geographic, 1983, 60 min.)

European & Asian Bear Ranges

Atlantic Ocean

FORMER SOVIET UNION

EUROPE

ASIA

Pacific Ocean

INDIA

MALAYSIA

- ASIAN BLACK BEAR
- EUROPEAN BROWN BEAR
- GIANT PANDA BEAR
- SUN BEAR
- SLOTH BEAR

WHERE TO SEE BEARS

Zoos

Of the more than 300 zoos worldwide, most exhibit at least one species. Polar bears are most common.

Parks and Wilderness Areas

Important: *Bears should be left undisturbed in their wilderness habitats.*

- McNeil River Sanctuary, Alaska – Four-day permits are chosen by lottery. Resident biologists act as guides and interpreters. Many naturalists and photographers rank this as one of the world's best wildlife-viewing areas.

- Katmai National Park, Alaska – Watch bears fish from an elevated platform at Brooks Falls. Rangers explain safety rules. The park's 600 brown bears have the right-of-way at all times.

- Churchill, Canada – This town on Hudson Bay offers tundra buggy tours to see polar bears congregating in the area each fall.

- Bears may be seen in several U.S. national parks including Denali in Alaska, Glacier in Montana, Great Smoky Mountains in Tennessee, and Yellowstone in Wyoming.

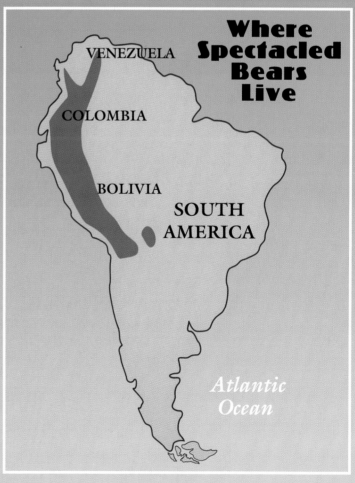

Where Spectacled Bears Live

VENEZUELA

COLOMBIA

BOLIVIA

SOUTH AMERICA

Atlantic Ocean

CLOSE-UP
A Focus on Nature

Here's what teachers, parents, kids, and nature lovers of all ages say about this series:

• • • • • • • •

"High-interest topics, written in grownup language yet clear enough for kids..."

"Dazzling, detailed photos. Your beautiful books have a strong educational component—keep it up!"

"Packed with facts and priced right for busy adults."

"Extremely useful for students with reading difficulties..."

"Your book is the best souvenir we could have of our whale-watching trip."

"These books are great gift items for all the bird-watchers, divers, and wildlife artists on my list!"

Silver Burdett Press books are widely available at bookstores and gift outlets at museums, zoos, and aquaria throughout the U.S. and abroad. Educators and individuals wishing to order may also do so by writing directly to:

SILVER BURDETT PRESS
299 JEFFERSON ROAD,
PARSIPPANY, NJ 07054

◆ HABITATS ◆

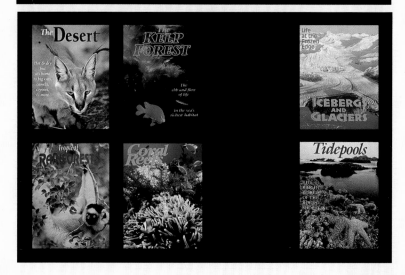

◆ ANIMALS ◆ BIG & SMALL

◆ BIRDS ◆ IN THE WILD

◆ MARINE LIFE ◆

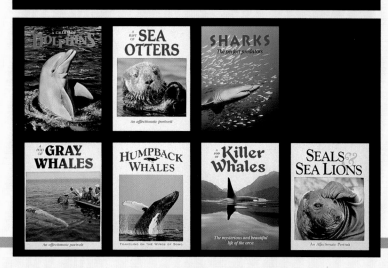

*Powerful symbol of nature,
yet vulnerable to threats
from civilization.*

*Of the eight bear species,
seven are endangered,
one threatened.*